# THE GLORY IS HERE

WILLIAM HATFIELD

Copyright © 2019 WILLIAM HATFIELD

All rights reserved.

ISBN: 978-1-7750330-6-6

## ACKNOWLEDGEMENTS

We are all on a journey through life! I want to thank all my family and friends who stand besides me and encourage me when times are tough.

I especially want to thank my aunt Viola for all her work in editing and preparing the manuscript of my first book for publishing. The knowledge she shared will help me to continue writing.

# DEDICATION

I dedicate this book to the thirsty and hungry saints of God that desire an intimacy with the Holy Spirit like no other. My prayer is that you can find this journey as a source of encouragement, strength and power to overcome life's struggles and walk in a greater sense of freedom and relationship with the Holy Spirit and all within your sphere of influence.

# PROLOGUE

There is a remnant in this generation that is tired of religion and the status quo. We are tired of going to church to meet man. We want to meet God. We want more of God or is it God wants more of us? This is my exploration of this situation

WILLIAM HATFIELD

# CONTENTS

Acknowledgments
Dedication

| | | |
|---|---|---|
| 1 | INTERERSTING TIMES | Pg. 7 |
| 2 | THE MANIFESTED PRESENCE OF GOD | Pg. 14 |
| 3 | THE GLORY OF THE LORD IN THE OLD TESTAMENT | Pg. 23 |
| 4 | HONOR AND GLORY | Pg. 28 |
| 5 | THE GLORY OF THE LORD IN THE NEW TESTAMENT | Pg. 33 |
| 6 | FROM THE GRAVEYARD TO THE GLORY | Pg. 47 |
| 7 | MANIFESTATIONS OF THE GLORY OF THE LORD IN OUR CHURCHES | Pg. 67 |
| 8 | MY TESTIMONY | Pg. 78 |
| 9 | EPILOGUE | Pg. 87 |
| 10 | ABOUT THE AUTHOR | Pg. 88 |

# 1 INTERESTING TIMES

We are living in interesting and perilous times! According to the bible we are living in the last days.

Acts 2:17-21 King James Version (KJV)

**17** And it shall come to pass in the last days, saith God; I will pour out of my Spirit upon all flesh: and your sons and your daughters shall prophesy, and your young men shall see visions, and your old men shall dream dreams:

**18** And on my servants and on my handmaidens I will pour out in those days of my Spirit; and they shall prophesy:

**19** And I will shew wonders in heaven above, and signs in the earth beneath; blood, and fire, and vapor of smoke:

**20** The sun shall be turned into darkness, and the moon into blood, before the great and notable day of the Lord come:

**21** And it shall come to pass, that whosoever shall call on the name of the Lord shall be saved.

LUKE 4:18 The Spirit of the Lord *is* upon me, because he hath anointed me to preach the gospel to the poor; he hath sent me to heal the broken-hearted, to preach deliverance to the captives, and recovering of sight to the blind, to set at liberty them that are bruised,

19 To preach the acceptable year of the Lord.

Isaiah 61: 1 The Spirit of the Lord GOD *is* upon me; because the LORD hath anointed me to preach good tidings unto the meek; he hath sent me to bind up the broken-hearted, to proclaim liberty to the captives, and the opening of the prison to *them that are* bound;

2 To proclaim the acceptable year of the LORD, and the day of vengeance of our God; to comfort all that mourn;

3 To appoint unto them that mourn in Zion, to give unto them beauty for ashes, the oil of joy for mourning, the garment of praise for the spirit of heaviness; that they might be called trees of righteousness, the planting of the LORD, that he might be glorified.

**I believe the last days started when Jesus preached this message. I personally think the**

term last days refers to the time of the gentiles being fulfilled. The times of the gentiles are when God is moving to bring in non-Jews to His kingdom. This is also known as the church age when Israel is in partial blindness when God is moving by His Spirit to bring all peoples of the earth into the saving knowledge of Jesus Christ, not just Israelis but all peoples. Notice in Luke where Jesus quoted Isaiah, he stopped at acceptable day of the Lord and never included the day of vengeance of our God. I believe the day of vengeance is future after this church age or time of the gentiles or time of grace comes to a close. Notice in acts; the day of the Lord; and Isaiah; the day of vengeance of our God. These two statements are referring to the same event known in Jeremiah, Matthew and Romans.

## Jeremiah 30:4-8
Now these *are* the words that the LORD spoke concerning Israel and Judah. "For thus says the LORD:
'We have heard a voice of trembling,
Of fear, and not of peace.
Ask now, and see,
Whether a man is ever in labor with child?
So why do I see every man *with* his hands on his loins

Like a woman in labor,
And all faces turned pale?
Alas! For that day *is* great,
So that none *is* like it;
And it *is* the time of Jacob's trouble,
But he shall be saved out of it.
'For it shall come to pass in that day,'
Says the LORD of hosts,
'*That* I will break his yoke from your neck,
And will burst your bonds;
Foreigners shall no more enslave them.

## Matthew 24:21-22

For then there will be great tribulation, such as has not been since the beginning of the world until this time, no, nor ever shall be. And unless those days were shortened, no flesh would be saved; but for the elect's sake those days will be shortened.

- ## Romans 1:18-27

For the wrath of God is revealed from heaven against all ungodliness and unrighteousness of men, who suppress the truth in unrighteousness, because what may be known of God is manifest in them, for God has shown *it* to them. For since the creation of the world His invisible *attributes* are clearly seen, being understood by the things that are made, *even* His eternal power and Godhead, so that they are without excuse, because, although they knew God, they did not glorify *Him* as God, nor were thankful, but became futile in their thoughts, and their foolish hearts were darkened. Professing to be wise, they became fools, and changed the glory of the incorruptible God into an image made like corruptible man—and birds and four-footed animals and creeping things. Therefore God also gave them up to uncleanness, in the lusts of their hearts, to dishonor their bodies among themselves, who exchanged the truth of God for the lie, and worshiped and served the creature rather than the Creator, who is blessed forever. Amen. For this reason God gave them up to vile passions. For even their women exchanged the natural use for what is against nature. Likewise also the men, leaving the natural use of the woman, burned in their lust for one another, men with men committing what is shameful, and receiving in themselves the penalty of their error which was due.

But before the day of vengeance is the acceptable year of the Lord which is Isaiah 61: 3 To appoint unto them that mourn in Zion, to give unto them beauty for ashes, the oil of joy for mourning, the garment of praise for the spirit of heaviness; that they might be called trees of righteousness, the planting of the LORD, that he might be glorified.

We are in the day of glorifying God in our own personal lives and receiving His glory to fulfill Isaiah 61:3 in our personal lives and the corporate lives of the body of Christ. Don't get religious at this point on me and say God doesn't share his glory with any man. God's Glory as in praise and worship is not now or never going to a man. Jesus in John 17:22 And the glory which thou gavest me I have given them; that they may be one, even as we are one: King James Bible. The word Glory in this scripture is referring to the Holy Spirit which was given after Jesus rose from the dead and was glorified and sits at the right hand of God the Father. The Holy Spirit was poured out on the day of Pentecost. From that day forward all people who are born again and received the Holy Spirit are now candidates for the manifestations of the Holy Spirit and the manifest presence of God the Father.

Even though the Day of the Lord, the Day of vengeance, time of Jacobs trouble and the book of revelation are basically the same event and is an interesting study. I will let that happen another time. I am interested in the Glory of the Lord; I want to know Him, submit myself to Him, and experience Him daily. I want to experience the manifested presence of the Father God to see Isaiah 61:3 fulfilled in my life. When Isaiah 61:3 is fulfilled in my life I believe I will experience
**Revelation 3:10-11**
Because you have kept My command to persevere, I also will keep you from the hour of trial which shall come upon the whole world, to test those who dwell on the earth. Behold, I am coming quickly! Hold fast what you have, that no one may take your crown.

## 2 THE MANIFESTED PRESENCE OF GOD

What does it mean to manifest God's glory? When **God's glory** manifests in a man's life, it **means God** is exalted in such a life. To **manifest means** to show forth, to reveal, to unveil, to make known, to exhibit, to authenticate or to notarize. Therefore, to **manifest** the **glory** of **God means** to demonstrate the power of the spirit of **God**.

HOW DO YOU EXALT GOD IN YOUR LIFE? I believe of course the first step of exalting God in your life is to move from religion to relationship. There are many sincere people in the body of Christ who were truly born again but have decided a religion of does and don'ts with legalistic thinking is the proper way for them. You can find this attitude amongst denominations and empire builders. Empire builders will build their particular organization in order to get notoriety and fame and let the whole world know they are the latest and greatest move of God in the earth. Empire builders will only accept people that fit their agendas.

To be a true kingdom of God builder you will accept everybody and Love on them and help them to find their destinies in Christ and encourage them to grow and fulfill their destinies. Relationships go both ways horizontal and vertical. Horizontal is up, the fellowship between you and God. Vertical is in front of you between others within your sphere of influence. I personally believe the relationships you have with other people is actually a telltale sign of the relationship you have with the Holy Spirit. When you have an intimate and close relationship with the Holy Spirit it will become evident in your relationship with people. Galatians 5 is a good passage to read. I have found by studying this passage, meditating and praying about then trying to walk it out in my life has given me victory to exalt God and allow him to manifest Himself through me.

Galatians 5:16 This I say then, Walk in the Spirit, and ye shall not fulfil the lust of the flesh.

**17** For the flesh lusteth against the Spirit, and the Spirit against the flesh: and these are contrary the one to the other: so that ye cannot do the things that ye would.

**18** But if ye be led of the Spirit, ye are not under the law.

**19** Now the works of the flesh are manifest, which are these; Adultery, fornication, uncleanness, lasciviousness,

**20** Idolatry, witchcraft, hatred, variance, emulations, wrath, strife, seditions, heresies,

**21** Envying's, murders, drunkenness, revelling's, and such like: of the which I tell you before, as I have also told you in time past, that they which do such things shall not inherit the kingdom of God.

**22** But the fruit of the Spirit is love, joy, peace, longsuffering, gentleness, goodness, faith,

**23** Meekness, temperance: against such there is no law.

**24** And they that are Christ's have crucified the flesh with the affections and lusts.

**25** If we live in the Spirit, let us also walk in the Spirit.

**26** Let us not be desirous of vain glory, provoking one another, envying one another.

When I looked at the fruit of the Spirit and prayed about it I realized if I develop it in my life I will I will not only be exalting God but I can be in a position to encourage and strengthen people with the gifts God has placed in my life. By doing this I am allowing God's Glory to be manifested according to the submission I give to His authority and Love I accept in my life. The greater the revelation of His Love and authority; the greater the manifestation of His Glory through my life to others. One key I found was that it's not about me. When I got over self-centered and selfishness I enjoyed more peace and freedom in my relationship with God and people. By developing the fruit of the Spirit in your life you not only live in the Spirit but you walk in the Spirit which is a lifestyle which you have committed yourself to.

When I looked at the fruit of the Spirit I decided to develop the first three for myself. Love, Joy and peace: If I can't love myself and accept who God made me to be, how can I accept and love others? If I am down and depressed and never experience Joy in my life, why would anybody want what I got? The same goes for peace if I am stressed out and in turmoil over circumstances and situations my life is chaotic and not a witness to anyone. Now this is where life becomes interesting because in your pursuit of love, joy and peace you may come against things that are buried deep in your subconscious that prevents you from developing in this area. One sign of deeper issues is if you have a continual repeating thought process over a bad situation or somebody that has did you harm physically or emotionally. This is a sure notification you need the help of others in your life. In a strong bible based church you should be able to find a deliverance team to help you. I am not saying you are demon possessed but that your soul is oppressed in order to prevent you from going deeper into God's Glory. I will share my experience in this matter in the chapter from the graveyard to Glory.

The next three longsuffering, gentleness, and goodness I develop in my life for others. Longsuffering is not as some denominations teach that you are to tolerate sickness and endure until God might heal you if it is His will and you will give him glory through your suffering pain and anguish. Longsuffering is when you are dealing with people and because of spiritual blindness they can't see the answer to the problems they are experiencing. They reject you and may say negative things but you won't take offence from them. You will walk in gentleness because Proverbs 15 King James Version (KJV) **15** A soft answer turneth away wrath: but grievous words stir up anger.

² The tongue of the wise useth knowledge aright: but the mouth of fools poureth out foolishness. So by walking in gentleness you deflate the situation and help them to take a closer look at the answer you are presenting them.

By not taking offence (longsuffering) and giving soft answer (gentleness) you are allowing the goodness of God to be manifested in your life to others.
**Romans 2:4** King James Version (KJV)
⁴ Or despisest thou the riches of his goodness and forbearance and longsuffering; not knowing that the goodness of God leadeth thee to repentance?

Repentance will usually cure or solve a lot if issues we are going through in our lives. If God is using you to help people or you have a desire to help people be free to walk in the Spirit and manifest God's Glory in their lives develop these three fruit of the Spirit in your life.

The last three: faith, meekness, temperance, I develop in my life for God. What do you mean for

God? God doesn't need anything He is all sufficient. True but I am not. Let me explain. Say the Holy Spirit begins talking to you about the gifts or manifestations of the Holy Spirit.

1 Corinthians 12 King James Version (KJV)

**12** Now concerning spiritual gifts, brethren, I would not have you ignorant.

² Ye know that ye were Gentiles, carried away unto these dumb idols, even as ye were led.

³ Wherefore I give you to understand, that no man speaking by the Spirit of God calleth Jesus accursed: and that no man can say that Jesus is the Lord, but by the Holy Ghost.

⁴ Now there are diversities of gifts, but the same Spirit.

⁵ And there are differences of administrations, but the same Lord.

⁶ And there are diversities of operations, but it is the same God which worketh all in all.

⁷ But the manifestation of the Spirit is given to every man to profit withal.

⁸ For to one is given by the Spirit the word of wisdom; to another the word of knowledge by the same Spirit;

⁹ To another faith by the same Spirit; to another the gifts of healing by the same Spirit;

¹⁰ To another the working of miracles; to another prophecy; to another discerning of spirits; to another divers kinds of tongues; to another the interpretation of tongues:

¹¹ But all these worketh that one and the selfsame Spirit, dividing to every man severally as he will.

¹² For as the body is one, and hath many members, and all the members of that one body, being many, are one body: so also is Christ

    The Holy Spirit wants to use you in the speaking gifts tongues, interpretation of tongues or prophecy. Maybe the revelation gifts word of wisdom, word of knowledge, discerning of spirits, or the power gifts faith, gifts of healing, working of miracles. Just a note here faith here is a supernatural gift where there is absolutely no doubt or unbelief in any form present. Why **faith, meekness, temperance?** Faith that God is manifesting Himself through you and He has found you a vessel of honor to manifest His Glory through. Meekness because it's not about you.

I've heard many people say they have the gift of Healing to heal certain diseases and people who have those sicknesses leave in the same shape they came in with even after the person who claimed they had the gift prayed for them. I wonder why? Per chance the minister is claiming something that's not his belongs to him. Meekness says it's all about the Holy Spirit and not me. Temperance is moderation in thought, word, or action. Those who practice temperance are self-controlled and show restraint in their passions and behaviors. In other words when God is manifesting Himself through your life you are not taking the credit saying look what I did expecting accolades thus enjoying vain glory. It's all about Jesus not about me. This my readers is what I believe is how to exalt God in our lives.

# 3 THE GLORY OF THE LORD IN THE OLD TESTAMENT

One such puzzling word found in several verses of the **Old Testament** is "**glory**" (Hebrew kawbode). The word **glory** is used 148 times in Genesis, Exodus, Leviticus and Numbers, and from Deuteronomy to Malachi. ... Psalms 62:7: "In **God** is my salvation and my **glory**." Jeremiah 13:16: "Give **glory** to the **Lord** your **God**."

Abode
[əˈbōd]
NOUN
*formal*
*literary*
1. a place of residence; a house or home. "my humble abode" ·

    *synonyms:*
    home · house · place of residence/habitation · accommodation · habitat ·
    [more]
    - residence.
      "a place of abode"

- *archaic*
  a stay; a sojourn.

Psalm 62:7 King James Version (KJV)
⁷ In God is my salvation and my glory: the rock of my strength, and my refuge, is in God.

Meaning of kawbode

glory, honor, glorious, abundance

1. abundance, riches
2. honor, splendor, glory
3. honor, dignity
4. honor, reputation
5. honor, reverence, glory
6. glory

By these meanings we see God's desire to not only to visit with His people and have occasional FELLOWSHIP but wanted permanent home to live with his people. Being only carnal or natural man the Israelites desire was to build God a temple so they could go visit and get their sins covered by the blood of animals to bring God's goodness to their nation and homes. This was a relationship at arm's length and when they walked in the lust of the flesh which was easier to do than follow

rules and regulations and follow false god's a prophet was raised up to warn them. **Jeremiah 13:16** [16]Give glory to the LORD your God before he brings the darkness, before your feet stumble on the darkening hills. You hope for light, but he will turn it to utter darkness and change it to deep gloom.
Jeremiah 13:16. Give glory to the Lord — That is to say, "Confess your faults, and humble yourselves under his mighty hand, before he bring upon you the night of affliction; before the time come, when ye shall be forced to fly by night unto the mountains for fear of the enemy."

No matter how you look at it there is a place of submission and repentance to experience the Glory (kawbode) of God. Even in the new testament if we serve ourselves and walk in the lust of our flesh we will be in utter darkness and deep gloom. What the old testament people and sad to say many new testament believers in Jesus Christ don't understand is, God is not sitting in heaven waiting to bring bad stuff on you if you fail or get out of line. He set laws in motion at creation and when Moses brought down the ten commandments and wrote the additional by laws. These work by cause and effect, jump off a roof and you hit the ground thus proving the law of gravity works. God didn't send an angel telling him to knock you to the ground because I don't Want him to float in the air. In the same sense the laws of God work without Him being there to enforce them.

The soul that sins shall die. To put it another way, to save your soul, your life, you must live a godly life. The more we sin, the more we invite our own deaths. While death may well not be immediate, sin clearly never pays. This theme is prevalent in the Book of Proverbs. Over and over again we read statements like the following: "The fear of the Lord prolongs days, but the years of the wicked will be shortened" (Prov 10:27). "In the way of righteousness there is life, and in its pathway there is no death" (Prov 12:28). "Evil pursues sinners" (Prov 13:21). "The fear of the Lord is a fountain of life, to turn one away from the snares of death" (Prov 14:27). "Harsh discipline is for him who forsakes the way, and he who hates correction will die" (Prov 15:10). "He who sows iniquity will reap sorrow" (Prov 22:8). For the believer, as well as for the unbeliever, sin never pays.

When you walk in the fear of the Lord you will experience the kawbode of the Lord and He will live with you not just show up occasionally to visit.

# 4 **HONOR AND GLORY**

Meaning of kawbode

Glory, honor, glorious, abundance

1. abundance, riches
2. honor, splendor, glory
3. honor, dignity
4. honor, reputation
5. honor, reverence, glory
6. glory

    When you look at Kawbode and one of the meanings is honor, you begin to wonder about the North American culture? From my experiences with people and church organizations it seems like a me generation. To many preachers, people and denominations want honor but refuse to give honor to their congregation or other people because of perception and exaltation of self. I think I am awesome great and important therefore honor me and feel privilege that I talk to you because look at what I have done and what did you do that I should honor you? I have even imparted upon myself a title and if you don't address me by my title I won't talk to you.

I am not saying all churches are like this God forbid that I would make such a foolish judgment. The church I am presently attending is an awesome example of a church organization of honoring all people. The leadership is humble and caring. They realize they are part of the Body of Christ and the Holy Spirit has placed abilities and talents and gifts in their lives. They use their abilities to build the rest of the Body in love and help us find our place in the kingdom of God. Honor in this church flows both ways; from the congregation to the leadership and from the leadership to the congregation.

Philippians 2:3 World English Bible (WEB)

³ doing nothing through rivalry or through conceit, but in humility, each counting others better than himself;

When you honor the gift of God: a born again Spirit filled Christian who has a gift in him which Is Jesus Christ and the Holy Spirit and life and is God's gift to the world **you honor God** who redeemed that individual.

    I was in the Philippians in 2015 for the month of March and I was able to share a message on the fruit of the Spirit in a couple of bible colleges and a few churches. I noticed a culture of honor in that nation which totally impressed me. They even called me a great theologian which surprised me because I am just a construction worker that loves to share the revelation I have of Jesus. I have only one title and that is my name. My name is William and I use whatever abilities and talents God gives me to bring encouragement and exhortation to the body of Christ.

My personal opinion is that if our churches become places of honor and kingdom builders; rather than empire builders and fame seekers, we would see a major move of the Glory of God across our nation.

We are all equal in the body of Christ no one is greater than the other. We have different abilities and talents that we use to bless others but no one is greater. Let me share an experience I had with God to prove this. I believe this experience can be for anyone and everyone. I was sitting in my chair reading a book when I read the phrase GOD NEEDS YOU. I laughed and said God you don't need me you have…. I mentioned Pastors and famous preachers and evangelists thinking you have them what do you need with me. I suddenly went into a trance and everything around me disappeared. I was sitting beside a creek and Jesus was standing in front of me. He reached down in front of me and picked a small rough looking pebble from the creek bed. He said you are this pebble I am going to grind you polish you and make you shine then I am going to put you back in the creek. The creek would not be complete without you. I NEED YOU. I came out of that trance with a new value of myself and a GREATER LOVE FOR GOD.

WE HONOR EVERYONE BUT DON'T DEMEAN YOURSELF BECAUSE WE ALL HAVE A PLACE AND PURPOSE THAT IS NEEDED BY OTHERS.

# 5 THE GLORY OF THE LORD IN THE NEW TESTAMENT

There are times in the history of God's dealing with humanity when the wall between the human world of time and space and the invisible, supernatural world of God and angels becomes paper-thin. That's when angels appear. Think of Jacob's dream of a ladder connecting heaven and earth with angels walking up and down. God, at the top of the ladder, begins speaking to him, renewing the promises made to his grandfather Abraham and father Isaac. Upon awakening in the morning Jacob declared, *"What an awesome place this is! It is none other than the house of God, the very gateway to heaven!"* (Gen. 28:17 NLT).

Fast-forward more than a millennium and a half to a starry night in the countryside below the village of Bethlehem where shepherds were watching their sheep. Luke, the only Gentile author in the Bible, tells the story:

> *"Suddenly, an angel of the Lord appeared among them, and the radiance of the Lord's glory surrounded them. They were terrified, but the angel reassured them. 'Don't be afraid!' he said. 'I bring you good news that will bring great joy to all people. The Savior—yes, the Messiah, the Lord—has been born today in Bethlehem, the city of David! And you will recognize him by this sign: You will find a baby wrapped snugly in strips of cloth, lying in a manger.' Suddenly, the angel was joined by a vast host of others—the armies of heaven—praising God and saying,*
>
> > *'Glory to God in highest heaven,*
> >
> > *and peace on earth to those with whom God is pleased.'"* (Luke 2:9-14 NLT).

Finally, Matthew takes us to a little mountaintop where Jesus had taken his closest disciples, Peter, James and John. Here the allusions to Moses and Mount Sinai are meant to strike the reader:

> *"As the men watched, Jesus' appearance was transformed so that his face shone like the sun, and his clothes became as white as light. Suddenly, Moses and Elijah appeared and began talking with Jesus. Peter exclaimed, 'Lord, it's wonderful for us to be here! If you want, I'll make three shelters as memorials—one for you, one for Moses, and one for Elijah.' But even as he spoke, a bright cloud overshadowed them, and a voice from the cloud said, 'This is my dearly loved Son, who brings me great joy. Listen to him.' The disciples were terrified and fell face down on the ground. Then Jesus came over and touched them. 'Get up,' he said. 'Don't be afraid.' And when they looked up, Moses and Elijah were gone, and they saw only Jesus. As they went back down the mountain, Jesus commanded them, "Don't tell anyone what you have seen until the*

*Son of Man has been raised from the dead"* (Mat. 17:2-9 NLT).

2 CORINTHIANS 3: [18] and we all, who with unveiled faces contemplate the Lord's glory, are being transformed into his image with ever-increasing glory, which comes from the Lord, who is the Spirit.

There is a big difference between God's glory being manifested in the Old Testament and the New Testament. In the old testament when God chose to show up He covered himself in a dark cloud so as to not destroy the people he wanted to talk to. This was after Moses gave the law of God. Before Moses in Abraham's time it was a dispensation of promise and it seemed God could show up easier and deal with mankind. We in the New Testament, after accepting Jesus as savior and being born again and not under the condemnation of the law, are free to experience God's glory to a greater degree.

2 Corinthians 5:21 World English Bible (WEB)
[21] For him who knew no sin he made to be sin on our behalf; so that in him we might become the righteousness of God.

Jesus took our sin and gave US the righteousness of God.

1 John 3:9 whoever is born of God doesn't commit sin, because his seed remains in him; and he can't sin, because he is born of God.
- *World English Bible*

> *"If the old way, which brings condemnation, was glorious, how much more glorious is the new way, which makes us right with God! In fact, that first glory was not glorious at all compared with the overwhelming glory of the new way . . . We are not like Moses, who put a veil over his face so the people of Israel would not see the glory, even though it was destined to fade away. But the people's minds were hardened, and to this day whenever the old covenant is being read, the same veil covers their minds so*

*they cannot understand the truth. And this veil can be removed only by believing in Christ . . . But whenever someone turns to the Lord, the veil is taken away. For the Lord is the Spirit, and wherever the Spirit of the Lord is, there is freedom. So all of us who have had that veil removed can see and reflect the glory of the Lord. And the Lord—who is the Spirit—makes us more and more like him as we are changed into his glorious image"* (II Cor. 3:9-10; 13-14; 16-18 NLT).

*Jesus and the Holy Spirit who is the glory of God resides in the born again believer. We don't expect for God's glory to come upon us as in the old testament, but at times it does. God's glory resides in us so he should come out of us manifesting in the natural world bringing signs and wonders.*

## Mark 16:17-20 New King James Version (NKJV)

[17] And these signs will follow those who[a] believe: In My name they will cast out demons; they will speak with new tongues; [18] they[b] will take up serpents; and if they drink anything deadly, it will by no means

hurt them; they will lay hands on the sick, and they will recover."

# Christ Ascends to God's Right Hand

**19** So then, after the Lord had spoken to them, He was received up into heaven, and sat down at the right hand of God. **20** And they went out and preached everywhere, the Lord working with *them* and confirming the word through the accompanying signs. Amen.

God is continually working with us and on us. We are being changed from Glory to Glory. I believe that God's goal is to cause us to be like Jesus. He is working with our souls; prompting, guiding, exhorting us and helping us change in the image of Jesus.

### *Love Comes from God*
...**16**And we have come to know and believe the love that God has for us. God is love; whoever abides in love abides in God, and God in him. **17**In this way, love has been perfected among us, so that we may have confidence on the day of judgment; for in this world we are just like Him.

The church of God, the body of Christ is supposed to be in the image of Jesus Christ. We act like Him, we walk in His Love and the supernatural realm of the Spirit is not alien or foreign to us. We should be in a place where we could say "THE SUPERNATURAL IS MORE REAL TO US THAN THE NATURAL WORLD."

We are in the last hours of the last days and God is pouring out His Spirit on all flesh. Acts 2:**16**but this is what was spoken of through the prophet Joel:

**17**'AND IT SHALL BE IN THE LAST DAYS,' God says,
'THAT I WILL POUR FORTH OF MY SPIRIT ON ALL MANKIND;
AND YOUR SONS AND YOUR DAUGHTERS SHALL PROPHESY,
AND YOUR YOUNG MEN SHALL SEE VISIONS,
AND YOUR OLD MEN SHALL DREAM DREAMS;

**18**EVEN ON MY BONDSLAVES, BOTH MEN AND WOMEN,
I WILL IN THOSE DAYS POUR FORTH OF MY SPIRIT
And they shall prophesy.

**19** 'AND I WILL GRANT WONDERS IN THE SKY ABOVE
    AND SIGNS ON THE EARTH BELOW, BLOOD, AND FIRE, AND VAPOR OF SMOKE.

**20** 'THE SUN WILL BE TURNED INTO DARKNESS AND THE MOON INTO BLOOD, BEFORE THE GREAT AND GLORIOUS DAY OF THE LORD SHALL COME.

**21** 'AND IT SHALL BE THAT EVERYONE WHO CALLS ON THE NAME OF THE LORD WILL BE SAVED.'

In today's world we are all connected by the internet and you can see and hear things that God is doing throughout the earth. Now you have to judge some of the things you have seen and heard because there are many glory seekers, date setters and accolade seekers out there. God pouring out His spirit on you and bringing you into a greater dimension of the supernatural is not to make you famous and popular. Verse 21 shows you why. In this next move of God which I believe will bring Jesus appearing for the resurrection mentioned in 1 Corinthians 15:53-55.

I would like to share a vision I had concerning this move of God I believe is coming. I was at my cousins home. She was doing dishes so I sat in her living room waiting for her to finish so we could visit. I decided to stand and praise and worship the Lord. Suddenly I heard a large piercing whistle in my spirit which caused me to turn my head. When I did I was suddenly watching and event unfolding before my eyes. It was high definition and very clear to watch. I watched waves of the ocean coming into the shore and after a few waves I noticed one wave come a long way into the shore. It seemed like it came in further than the others. The when it began to go out, it never stopped. It kept going out further and further and my thought was who is draining the ocean? I noticed the ocean floor, it was clean. There was no garbage or sunken ships or any kind of pollution at all. TOTALLY CLEAN! So clean you could lay in it and enjoy a nice relaxing time without having to worry about a shower later. Then I felt and heard the earth began to rumble and quake. I looked across the ocean floor and in the distance I saw a huge tidal wave About three thousand feet tall coming to the shore and Jesus was riding the top of it.

My interpretation of the vision is quite simple. The waves represent moves of God. The shore represents humanity. We have seen many moves of God in the earth, even in our generation. People have various opinions about what God is doing in the earth and that is and can be expected. After all God created unique and wonderful people from no one classified mold. Psalm 139:14 I will give thanks to You, for I am fearfully and wonderfully made; Wonderful are Your works, And my soul knows it very well.

The wave that seemed to come into the shore further than the other waves, I believe is a wave of cleansing or holiness. I believe God wants to move through His Church the body of Christ in such a supernatural way that holiness and purity of the soul has to be dominate in the church. Our spirits are redeemed and perfect an d can't sin and our bodies are yet to be redeemed at the resurrection but our souls

( mind will emotions re in the processed of being saved.) Romans 12:1-2, **1**Therefore I urge you, brethren, by the mercies of God, to present your bodies a living and holy sacrifice, acceptable to God, *which is* your spiritual service of worship. **2**And do not be conformed to this world, but be transformed by the renewing of your mind, so that you may prove what the will of God is, that which is good and acceptable and perfect.  **1**Therefore I urge you, brethren, by the mercies of God, to present your bodies a living and holy sacrifice, acceptable to God, *which is* your spiritual service of worship. **2**And do not be conformed to this world, but be transformed by the renewing of your mind, so that you may prove what the will of God is, that which is good and acceptable and perfect.  **1**Therefore I urge you, brethren, by the mercies of God, to present your bodies a living and holy sacrifice, acceptable to God, *which is* your spiritual service of worship. **2**And do not be conformed to this world, but be transformed by the renewing of your mind, so that you may prove what the will of God is, that which is good and acceptable and perfect.  **1**Therefore I urge you, brethren, by the mercies of God, to present your bodies a living and holy sacrifice, acceptable to God, *which is* your spiritual service of worship. **2**And do not be conformed to this world, but be transformed by the renewing of your mind, so that you may prove what the will of God is, that which is good and acceptable and perfect.  **1**Therefore I urge you, brethren, by the mercies of God, to present your bodies a living and holy sacrifice, acceptable to God, *which is* your spiritual service of worship. **2**And do not be conformed to this world, but be transformed by the renewing of your mind, so that you may prove what the will of God is, that which is good and acceptable and perfect.  **1**Therefore I urge you, brethren, by the mercies of God, to present your bodies a living and holy sacrifice, acceptable to God, *which is* your spiritual service of worship. **2**And do not be conformed to this world, but be transformed by the renewing of your mind, so that you may prove what the will of God is, that which is good and acceptable and perfect.  **1**Therefore I urge you, brethren, by the mercies of God, to present your bodies a living and holy sacrifice, acceptable to God, *which is* your spiritual service of worship. **2**And do not be conformed to this world, but be transformed by the renewing of your mind, so that you may prove what the will of God is, that which is good and acceptable and perfect.

This next move of God is going to reach untold millions for Jesus if not billions. I believe God is straightening up the soul of the church to make it look good and like Jesus which will attract people, rather than the religious legalistic bondage forming group people perceive it as and push it away.

In another section I want to look at some of the issues of the soul that keeps people from moving forward in God's plan for their lives.

# 6 FROM THE GRAVEYARD TO THE GLORY

I am sharing this writing not as a fivefold minister or theologian but as a former construction worker working mainly as a shingle of roofs. I love God with all my heart and continue to search and grow in my relationship with Him. Being born again our hearts or spirits are made new and are sealed by the Holy Spirit and made perfect in the eyes of God. **1 John 3:9** ⁹Whosoever is born of God doth not commit sin; for his seed remaineth in him: and he cannot sin, because he is born of God.

I had a truck accident in 1997 and had a brain injury that took ten years to heal from. One day while I was going for a walk I started praising God and thanking Him that I had a spirit. Suddenly the Holy Spirit interrupted my praise and said, "If you had a spirit where would you keep it?" I was a bit mystified and begin to think; "hmmm, as I touched my stomach because I remembered a scripture out of your belly flows rivers of living waters. I touched my heart thinking out of the heart the mouth speaks. I even placed my hands on my hips touching my pockets. Finally I said I don't know. Where would I put it?"

The Spirit of God said, "You don't have a spirit. You are a spirit, you live in a body and you possess a soul." Wow what a revelation. I knew this fact before but because of the brain injury and post traumatic amnesia that followed there was much I had forgotten including many aspects of my life. In this chapter I want to look at our souls because our spirits are redeemed and perfected. Our bodies one day at the resurrection will be redeemed. **The Resurrection Body 1 Corinthians 12:**

[35] But someone will ask, "How are the dead raised? With what kind of body will they come?" [36] How foolish! What you sow does not come to life unless it dies. [37] When you sow, you do not plant the body that will be, but just a seed,

perhaps of wheat or of something else. [38] But God gives it a body as he has determined, and to each kind of seed he gives its own body. [39] Not all flesh is the same: People have one kind of flesh, animals have another, birds another and fish another. [40] There are also heavenly bodies and there are earthly bodies; but the splendor of the heavenly bodies is one kind, and the splendor of the earthly bodies is another. [41] The sun has one kind of splendor, the moon another and the stars another; and star differs from star in splendor.

[42] So will it be with the resurrection of the dead. The body that is sown is perishable, it is raised imperishable; [43] it is sown in dishonor, it is raised in glory; it is sown in weakness, it is raised in power; [44] it is sown a natural body, it is raised a spiritual body.

If there is a natural body, there is also a spiritual body. [45] So it is written: "The first man

Adam became a living being; the last Adam, a life-giving spirit. [46] The spiritual did not come first, but the natural, and after that the spiritual. [47] The first man was of the dust of the earth; the second man is of heaven. [48] As was the earthly man, so are those who are of the earth; and as is the heavenly man, so also are those who are of heaven. [49] And just as we have borne the image of the earthly man, so shall we bear the image of the heavenly man.

[50] I declare to you, brothers and sisters, that flesh and blood cannot inherit the kingdom of God, nor does the perishable inherit the imperishable. [51] Listen, I tell you a mystery: We will not all sleep, but we will all be changed— [52] in a flash, in the twinkling of an eye, at the last trumpet. For the trumpet will sound, the dead will be raised imperishable, and we will be changed. [53] For the perishable must clothe itself

with the imperishable and the mortal with immortality. ⁵⁴ When the perishable has been clothed with the imperishable, and the mortal with immortality, then the saying that is written will come true: "Death has been swallowed up in victory."

⁵⁵ "Where, O death, is your victory?

Where, O death is your sting?"

⁵⁶ The sting of death is sin and the power of sin is the law. ⁵⁷ But thanks be to God! He gives us the victory through our Lord Jesus Christ.

⁵⁸ Therefore, my dear brothers and sisters, stand firm. Let nothing move you. Always give yourselves fully to the work of the Lord, because you know that your labor in the Lord is not in vain.

Our spirit is redeemed and our body is to be redeemed at the resurrection mentioned above. The soul which is in the process of redemption is what I want to talk about now.

**Romans 12:1-2 A Living Sacrifice**

¹Therefore, I urge you, brothers and sisters, in view of God's mercy, to offer your bodies as a living sacrifice, holy and pleasing to God—this is your true and proper worship. ² Do not conform to the pattern of this world, but be transformed by the renewing of your mind. Then you will be able to test and approve what God's will is— his good, pleasing and perfect will.

Our soul is made up of three areas our mind our will and our emotions. Our soul is what keeps us current in this natural world. Our soul is what is effected and influenced by the world system in which we live. We are warned not to conform to the pattern of this world. How do we conform? We accept the conditioning of the world system not realizing Satan who is the prince of the power of the air is mostly in control of the influences and temptations. Satan seeks to captivate your soul to keep you from experiencing God's glory.

2 Timothy 2:26 King James Bible
and *that* they may recover themselves out of the

snare of the devil, who are taken captive by him at his will.

Satan through temptations causes you to accept the lust of the flesh unknowingly. By accepting the lusts of the flesh Satan can hinder your growth in the Lord. Satan can't prevent us from being born again but through temptation and putting hindrances in your soul he hopes to slow down this process.

**2 Corinthians 3:16-18 Transformed from Glory to Glory**


2 Corinthians 3:16-18 Transformed from Glory to Glory

Every believer in Jesus Christ is an open letter, a walking living advertisement, for Christ. It is an awesome responsibility because the world is watching and judging Christianity by our attitudes and actions.

You may ask who is adequate for such a responsibility? The apostle Paul declared, "It is He who is all—sufficient who has made me sufficient for this task." He always thought of God as making him adequate to live and minister the Christian life. Only the Holy Spirit can change our human nature, therefore God calls us to an intimate relationship with Himself. The new covenant we have with Christ produces in us a greater splendor that will never fade. He calls us to an ever-growing intimate love relationship with Himself that never fades away.

The Christian looks upon the unveiled, the unhidden glories of the Lord, and are transformed into the same image from glory to glory. It is through faith that we look upon Him and are changed y the Holy Spirit.

Where do we get our vision of Him? It is as we are occupied with Him in His Word. As we study the Bible we understand and comprehend what He is like.

Who are those individuals in the Bible who have seen the glory of the Lord and been transformed?

I have said all this to share my experiences with temptations of the soul. The things I share are common to all mankind because Satán can only tempt with what is common. **1 Corinthians 10:13 (ASV)** There hath no temptation taken you but such as man can bear: but God is faithful, who will not suffer you to be tempted above that ye are able; but will with the temptation make also the way of escape, that ye may be able to endure it.

This is what I mean by temptations. Example you become ill with a crippling disease and your spouse runs off with another person. The temptation is to get angry, bitter, hurt and want revenge. Definitely a lust of the flesh. Walking in love is far from our minds. Our feelings get hurt. Emotions are in turmoil and we see no solution and can't do anything about it ourselves so we bury it.

Men's and women's makeup are very different and unique. Men's mind and thinking patterns have been compared to a WAFFLE.

You notice the little squares. A man puts everything into these squares or boxes and deals with it one at a time. When he is done he places it back then goes to another section takes the thing out deals with it and then puts it back. This is how he lives his life. I personally believe from experience and a dream I had from the Holy Spirit that one of these squares or boxes is called the graveyard where all hurts and situations we don't know how to deal with are buried and have head stones to mark the grave and its contents. The dream I had was Jesus had a plow and was going through the graveyard and came to a tombstone that read hatred of men. I remembered that one because at that time in my life all my hurts have come from men. Relatives and preachers seem to have it out for me to never become what God wanted me to be. Continually put me down belittle me and make me feel inferior and unworthy. So with these circumstances prevalent in my life the temptation to hate men which is a lust of the flesh was strong in my life. In this dream the grave was overturned and Jesus appeared to me and I repented and then mentioned the name of a man I was having issues with and said that he declared that man's name before the Father and the angels in heaven. I realized that I was to stop judging according to the flesh and make righteous judgments of the spirit and love. I shared my dream with the fellow and it encouraged and blessed him greatly.

As I continue don't be tempted to make comments about some of the people who did me harm because you may unknowingly be the villain in somebodies life. I personally think we all have been the villain knowingly or unknowingly at some point in our lives. My prayer and hope is that as I share my life with you that you will grow and avoid some of the heartaches I experienced because of not having a revelation of the love of God for people in my life until in my late forties when I had a heavenly experience when I had a dream or was translated into heaven and watched the great white throne judgment and got a deep revelation of God's love for all mankind, sinner and saint.

Not to leave women out of the equation I learned that a woman's makeup is like a plate of spaghetti.

With women everything is connected and they can multitask at a far superior level than men. Women can deal with multiple things at once and everything is connected. A man doesn't understand where a woman thinking begins or ends because everything is connected to some degree. I believe one of these strings is a grave yard string. A person might make a comment to a woman and a flood of emotions come pouring out; that to a MAN IT'S TOTALLY IRRELEVANT. Maybe the emotional outburst was because she was thinking about the times when she was abused or hurt and the comment triggered the emotional response accidentally. The apostle Peter wrote: *Husbands, likewise, dwell with them with understanding, giving honor to the wife, as to the weaker vessel, and as being heirs together of the grace of life, that your prayers may not be hindered (<u>1 Peter 3:7</u>)*.

This just shows that we all need help in our souls in order to experience freedom to flow with the glory of God and be unhampered in our relationship with God and others. I dealt with a lot of rejection because my second wife only used me for her own agenda and when I was in the hospital getting surgery she never visited and made me take a greyhound bus home. Her attending a religious conference was more important than her husband. The temptation there was to take a spirit of rejection which I did and unknowingly buried it in the graveyard. I buried it and refused to deal with it in order to put out a positive attitude to other people.

    Other areas that bothered me was my writing ability. I love to write. I can express myself on paper more than I can public speaking or conversation. I shared my desire to write a book about the dreams God gave me to a certain pastor of a church I attended. This pastor cursed me telling me that I was full of pride. I stopped writing thinking it was wrong and I would be prideful if I continued. But what confused me was the head of his denomination wrote many books and he promoted them over the pulpit. What I couldn't understand is that if I was prideful for wanting to write one book why weren't the heads of his denomination super prideful because they wrote many books? Why was his judgment on me different than his judgment on his denomination rulers? Another pastor shut me down when as a young Christian God began to use me in the gifts of the spirit. I went to him in excitement hoping to get affirmation and help in understanding about the manifestations of the spirit. What he said totally floored me, he said, "Why would God use you, when there is somebody like me around." Again an authority figure shut me down and made me feel unworthy for God to use.

I told this story to a friend of mine and she tried to encourage me by saying, "that's why God is using you because there is somebody like him around." I chuckled, but not before the unworthiness to be used by God and not value enough for God to give me anything was lodged in the graveyard. Actually the first time a pastor did something to hurt me was when I was ten years old. I attended a country Baptist church and an older girl by a couple of years sang a song. I thought the song was really good so I clapped my hands. The pastor came over and smacked my hands with a long pointer stick telling me to stop blaspheming God. That event left me with the attitude that showing appreciation for a job well done was wrong. Not knowing how to deal with it at ten years old it got buried in the graveyard. I left church and never returned until I was twenty one and had a supernatural experience with Jesus.

Let's go back further in my youth. I believe I was three or four years old when we went to visit my grandparents in Nova Scotia. I was put in bed one night and the lights were turned out. When my mother closed the bedroom door the closet door opened about a minute afterward. I watched what appeared as a ghost to a young boy and it came towards me. It got on my chest and put its hands around my throat and began choking me. I cried out for my mom and she came in. When I cried out the ghost went into my body so no one could see it. After explaining the event to my mother she just laughed and said there was no such things as ghost and I was just making it up because I didn't want to go to sleep.

My parents split up shortly after that because both my father and grandfather were sexual deviants. Being under authority of my father opened me up to that ghost which was pornographic spirit and it entered my soul. I was enticed by pornography for many years but when I started serving God I began to resist it and fight it. I was not alone in this area because statistics show many men saints and sinners deal with pornography. I would resist and get victory for long periods of time and then boom get sucked back in. I would condemn myself repent and get out and continue to resist again. This became a cycle of resistance, fall, self-condemnation, ask forgiveness then be free and resist when the temptation came around again.

    I finally got delivered when I attended a weekend course called ancient path ways at a church when I was forty years old. I am sharing this stuff to show you there is a battle for our souls. When we accepted Jesus, Satan lost the battle for our spirits which is the real you. Satan is after your soul to contaminate it to prevent you from experiencing God's Glory and having an intimate relationship with the Holy Spirit. If your soul which is your mind will and emotions is mixed up and damaged you will not be able to walk in the fruit of the spirit. You will suffer in your relationship with others and hold you back from receiving from God. The spirit of rejection, unworthiness, and self-condemnation kept me in bondage for many years. I went to a deliverance session at our church. Church in the vine, and the deliverance team helped me with these issues. I spent three hours in tears as we dealt with each situation the Holy Spirit revealed.

An interesting experienced happened to show me my value to God and the body of Christ. I was sitting in my chair reading a book when I read the phrase GOD NEEDS YOU. I laughed and said God you don't need me you have…. I mentioned Pastors and famous preachers and evangelists thinking you have them what do you need with me. I suddenly went into a trance and everything around me disappeared. I was sitting beside a creek and Jesus was standing in front of me. He reached down in front of me and picked a small rough looking pebble from the creek bed. He said you are this pebble I am going grind you polish you and make you shine then I am going to put you back in the creek. The creek would not be complete without you. I NEED YOU. I came out of that trance with a new value of myself and a GREATER LOVE FOR GOD. I don't have to receive my value from people only from Jesus. His shed blood didn't cover my sins but removed them from me as far as the east is from the west. I will no longer walk in self-condemnation because Jesus shed blood at the cross forgave and removed all sin from me past present and future. I will not condemn who Jesus forgave whether it's I or others.

I shared this part of my life to encourage you. If you have some things like what I went through haunting you in life. Don't be ashamed or fearful to seek help from people who will be confidential about your situation and only desires to see you free to walk in God's Glory. We will take another look at the soul later on. I just wanted to get this off my mind (soul) because what I went through in deliverance helped me incredibly. I hear people say if God would do this or that I would be better. What they don't realize is that at the cross Jesus accomplished everything you need to fulfill your destiny and have a good life and has deposited it in your spirit. It is the condition of your soul that is stopping you from receiving it in your body.

# 7 MANIFESTATIONS OF THE GLORY OF THE LORD IN OUR CHURCHES

According to theologians and prophecy experts we are in the last hours of the last days. According to theologians when Jesus was talking to the seven churches in revelation 2-3; we are in the time of the lukewarm church. Revelation 3:14-22 the Laodicean church. I have been to many denominational churches in my fifty plus years as a Christian. You enter the church and greeted by pastor's wife or ushers, find a seat and sit quietly. The musician or lucky enough the band comes to the stage. After a few words of encouragement they start their selection of music.

You sing to the best of your abilities not knowing the song but hope to follow the words on the projector screen hoping the projectionist keeps up. A quick gaze at the other members of the congregation reveals people standing like music leader asked but their lips are not moving. Always give grace and think maybe they just don't know the song and you continue to sing trying to get yourself in a spirit of worship. A few more songs and the musician hands it over to the guy doing announcements. You watch the musicians leave and get the impression of we entertained the saints for half an hour now it's the next guys turn. I have seen this with one man bands and in churches with multiple instruments and great charismatic singers. Spend an hour rocking the house with overbearing loud music and when they are done tell the congregation to give Jesus a clap offering for what He is about to do in the meeting.

Announcements are made then pastor comes up and begins his message. You try to follow along but find it not those exciting or even ministers to your heart. I think must be just me? You look around the congregation and notice chins resting on their chest eyes closed and breathing a bit heavy with the occasional snore. You actually begin to praise God silently that it's not just you.

The lukewarm church; empire builders and not kingdom builders. We got the money, talented musicians, light shows and we rock the house for Jesus. Seeker friendly in our preaching so as to not offend anyone in generation O for offence at everything. So funny to me on how we like to label each generation. My generation is called baby boomers. I call the generation 2019 generation O which is probably not the politically correct term but for the sake of discussion I used it.

The last church I served as associate pastor, I stepped down because the religious format was heading the way of cessations which is to say after the apostles died God stopped working with man accept to get him born again. After being born again you are on your own. Jesus doesn't baptize with the Holy Spirit with the evidence of speaking in tongues. There is no healing or miracles anymore. You come to church throw your money in a bucket listen to some guy in the pulpit go blah, blah, and blah. Don't hurt anyone and hope you make it to heaven when you die. My heart goes out to these people, in essence they are putting a literal sign over their church congregation and lives saying, "GOD YOU ARE NOT WELCOME HERE."

I was ordained in my spiritual father's fellowship and we would have services where a spirit of worship would come on the congregation and last three hours. Pastor's message was be blessed and see you for evening service. I was in one meeting where the Glory of God was so strong people's bodies seemed to vibrate, one gentleman came for prayer and the pastor began to minister to him. Suddenly under the inspiration of the Holy Spirit the pastor said, "Nobody touch this man." A woman approached with the attitude the pastor warning didn't include me. She put her had on the man's shoulder and she suddenly flew backwards ten feet into a wall and sat dazed wondering what happened. You may ask why that happened. I can only speculate that the Holy Spirit was doing a work in that man and wanted a man of humility ministering to him such was my spiritual father. We knew that woman very well; she was an attention getter always declaring look what I did.

When you go to church, whatever day of the week it is because you are going to meet God, not meet man. I enjoy the church I am currently fellowshipping in now. Church in the vine on 149 the ministry team from Pastor on down are true kingdom builders; full of honor, humility, grace and MOTIVATED BY AGAPE LOVE. The worship team doesn't entertain the saints but leads and encourages entering praise and worshiping thus attracting the Glory of God to manifest during the meeting. After the services there is a bit of afterglow or residue of glory so I decided to walk through the church congregation while people were getting ready to leave. Over by the far right wall were a couple praying for an individual, a few pews over words of encouragement spoken to another and out front a man was being delivered from demonic influence.

My personal belief is the personality of the church comes from the pastor character. The personality of church in the vine is people caring and ministering to people. I love and honor the leadership of this church. In my perspective there is no desire for vain glory and fame but wanting all within their sphere of influence to fulfill their destinies in Christ. They know they are limited in the natural and submit to the Holy Spirit guidance. You can have confidence with people who are not doing the work because of their greatness but allow the Holy Spirit who is the Glory of the Lord to work through them.

The thing that I enjoy that some people overlook is the Pastor or evangelist or guest speaker enter the pulpit it is as Jesus standing there sharing his heart. It's too easy to say HIM AGAIN heard him last week. When the manifested presence of God shows up to a meeting to fellowship with his children all are affected by it. The people who are hungry probably known as the remnant in this Laodicean age are going to experience the manifest presence of God more and more.

Joel 2:23 Be glad then, ye children of Zion, and rejoice in the LORD your God: for he hath given you the former rain moderately, and he will cause to come down for you the rain, the former rain, and the latter rain in the first month. 24 And the floors shall be full of wheat, and the fats shall overflow with wine and oil.

I believe this scripture is referring to the last hour of the last days out pouring of the Glory of the Lord. The former rain or manifestations of God in the old testament up to and including Jesus. The latter rain is from the day of Pentecost to our present time, the manifestations of the Glory of God in the earth. Both rains mixed together will cause a tsunami of God's Glory to fill the earth and reap an overwhelming harvest.

    I don't want to be a look Lou saying did you

hear or see what's going on over there? I want my soul in shape so I can be right in the middle with God using me as a vessel of honor.

## 2 Timothy 2:21 **King James Bible**

If a man therefore purge himself from these, he shall be a vessel unto honour, sanctified, and meet for the master's use, *and* prepared unto every good work.

## Christian Standard Bible

So if anyone purifies himself from anything dishonorable, he will be a special instrument, set apart, useful to the Master, prepared for every good work.

## Contemporary English Version

This is also how it is with people. The ones who stop doing evil and make themselves pure will become special. Their lives will be holy and pleasing to their Master, and they will be able to do all kinds of good deeds.

## Good News Translation

Those who make themselves clean from all those evil things, will be used for special purposes, because they are dedicated and useful to their Master, ready to be used for every good deed.

Submit to the Holy Spirit live a repentant life knowing it's not about you and watch The Glory of the Lord invade your life. I personally love when I experience the manifested presence of the Glory of the Lord. Each time I receive and experience a visitation I don't want Him to leave. I want to come to a place in my life where it's kawbode I am the dwelling place where the manifestations of the Glory of the Lord lives and where ever I go He goes. I guess you could say I am His mobile home and we travel together.

I have attended bible studies and church meetings when a spirit of laughter breaks out. not just a chuckle or smirk, but ugly hold your stomach belly laughing. I am pretty even keeled emotionally; I sit in peace while everyone laughs. I always wondered about this until I heard a preacher say, "joy is peace expressed and peace is joy at rest."

I asked a revivalist about it as it happened frequently during his meetings and he responded. "God is applying the anesthesia before the surgery." I liked this explanation because for God to release his Glory to the level He wants to in this last hour the church has to be free from sin. Our souls cannot be corrupted or we may see the Ananias and sapphira situation in our churches again. Another thing occurred to me was that I think we are seeing the mercy of God at work by Him not releasing the fullness of His Glory in our churches yet.

Here's another thought about the laughter in our churches and individuals. Psalm 2
**Contemporary English Version**

**The LORD's Chosen King**

1 Why do the nations plot,
and why do their people
 make useless plans?
2 The kings of this earth
 have all joined together
to turn against the LORD
 and his chosen king.
3 They say, "Let's cut the ropes

> and set ourselves free!"
> 4In heaven the LORD laughs
> as he sits on his throne,
> > making fun of the nations.
>
> Perchance God is manifesting his glory in the form of Laughter in our churches and individuals because He sees the final end of those who reject him and persecute his church the Body of Christ.

Being a Christian for over half a century my thinking has come to this; "I want more of God is not the issue but God wants more of us." We expect God to fit into our self-serving box and blame Him when things don't go our way. I am not full of doubt and unbelief it's that God stopped doing those things today. I can't speak for you but I know myself and I choose to be not self-deceived realizing most problems are in my soul and self-inflicted. MY PRAYER IS FATHER GOD HELP ME TO HAVE A PURE SOUL AND EXPERIENCE THE FULLNESS OF YOUR GLORY AND FULFILL MY DESTINY. WHEN I STAND AT THE BEMA SEAT OF CHRIST I WANT TO HEAR "WELL DONE ENTER INTO THE JOY OF THE LORD,."

## 8 MY TESTIMONY

## THE CALL

Unknown to me the Holy Spirit was planning a supernatural visitation as soon as the household had retired for the night.

Well into the early hours of the morning a light illuminating the interior of our house awakened me. Something was drawing me to the source of the light. As I walked into the kitchen I realized the light started outside radiating in. I was compelled into the porch and outside to the steps. The most marvelous sight I had ever seen appeared in the sky above me. A large pair of hands appeared in the sky held together in prayer. The hands began to open and a bible appeared. This bible was so huge it seemed to fill the entire sky. I stood in awe as a passage of scripture was circled.

The scripture was Ezekiel 3:10-11, "Moreover

He said to me: "Son of man, receive into your heart all my words that I speak to you, and hear with your ears. And go, get to the captives, to the children of your people, and speak to them and tell them, 'Thus says the Lord God,' whether they hear, or whether they refuse."

After a minute or so of watching this scene I was translated to the far end of my stepfather's grain field. My brothers and sisters were with me. We were standing beside the flat top hay wagon when Jesus appeared. He was wearing royal purple robes and radiated the most brilliant light I had ever seen. The glory radiating from Christ was so brilliant that creation ceased to exist, all you could see was Jesus and His glory, and nothing else was visible.

Jesus stood before us, His hand extended to us. In His hand was a piece of fruit of some sort. He presented this fruit to us, we all stood staring not sure what to do. I took the fruit from His hand and stood in amazement looking at this fruit, as it was not like anything we had ever seen. I decided to take a bite of the fruit. As soon as I bit off a piece of the fruit, the vision ended, I was sitting on the edge of my bed, daylight pouring in through the windows, wondering about the events that just took place.

I never really understood that vision as a child, but one thing was very clear to me; from that time on I wanted to be a minister of the Gospel of Jesus Christ. Life continued on for a young child, school during the week, work on the farm and Sunday school during the weekends. This lifestyle continued until I was fifteen and puberty set in and I experienced a new revelation. Girls now becoming young women, they were no longer funny looking boys to throw mud at and make fun of, but someone you wanted to impress in the worst way.

I moved out of home and to my uncle's house as my family was falling apart. My mother and step father were having marriage problems and would eventually divorce. I spent the next few years travelling around British Columbia, Alberta and Saskatchewan. I found a beautiful woman and married her and had a son. We were in the process of settling down to a quiet life and raising children. Christianity and religion was not part of our life even though my wife had mentioned that she used to go to Sunday school when she was a little girl.

We had what we thought was a normal Canadian lifestyle, full time job with a pay cheque every two weeks, then a time of relaxation partying with friends. My cousin showed up one evening while we had a small party going on and he asked my wife and me if we would baby sit his son while him and his wife went out for a time of relaxation. We agreed and my cousin asked if he could talk to me privately, sure I said. We went into the bedroom and he began to tell me about Jesus, His soon return and end of the age. I would just nod at him and say something like oh yeah okay just to get him out because I wanted to get back to my party.

My cousin came by many times to tell me about Jesus return and the end of the age. You know the crazy thing about it was; my cousin may have been doing a great job of sharing the gospel, but all I heard was, "Jesus is coming back and the earth is going to blow up and we are all going to die."

The spring of 1982 was a turning Point in my life, which would

Also affect the lives of others around me. Little did I realize that though?

I walked away from Jesus; HE never walked away from me. In April of 1982 Jesus visited me for the second time. This Visitation caused me to return to the Lord Jesus Christ with a fervent zealousness that still continues in my heart today.

The visitation started with the following scenes taking place: My fellow workers from the muffler shop and I were partying at a Southern American colonial style mansion. There was an abundance of drinking and carousing. I was participating fully when all of a sudden something started to bother my spirit. I did not understand what was happening, but I knew I had to ask God to forgive me for the lifestyle I had indulged in. Seeking privacy, I exited to a balcony overlooking a garden. I started to repent and tell God that I was sorry when I heard a voice say, "Forget it" I was startled and looked around to see who was playing a joke on me. Not finding anyone I continued to ask God's forgiveness. Again I heard a voice say, "Forget it." I looked around a second time, finding no one. This time I was compelled to look into the sky. As I watched the sky an amazing thing happened.

A strange but beautiful presence surrounded me as I watched the clouds change shapes. The clouds changed into a variety of different animals. A voice filled with love and peace spoke from among the animal shaped clouds. In my heart I knew I was talking with God. The voice proceeded to say, "Forget it, I want you to listen to my son Jesus, and if you can't make it grab onto one of the animals and it will bring you to heaven where you belong."[1]

I reached up and grabbed the leg of the closest animal, which happened to be a lamb. Suddenly, I found myself running along a vast expanse of beach. Beautiful, peaceful, and exhilarating was this place was in. I looked out over a huge ocean and was aware that everything I could see was created just for me. I was totally amazed at surroundings, especially the peace I experienced.

Suddenly I was removed from that place and a new scene unfolded before my eyes. I could see a Jesus, standing beside a large rock, watching over his sheep. I watched this scene with interest for few minutes. This scene disappeared and I was back at the balcony looking into the sky.

Again the voice of the Lord spoke to me saying, "Forget it, all I want you to do is listen to my Son." At this point I made an unbelieving arrogant statement toward God. Why you might ask would a person make arrogant statements toward God. It is quite simple; being influenced in the occult and street gangs you are taught how to rebel against all authority. To my surprise He responded with authority and sternness, I sensed that if I didn't stop being ignorant my life could be easily finished at that point Even though God responded with sternness the great love He has for His creation never left His voice. Adamantly the Lord said, "LISTEN TO MY SON JESUS." After this statement the visitation ended.

1: Jesus was not telling me to forget about repentance. He

      Was referring to my former lifestyle along with the guilt

      And fear. By saying forget it He was telling me that He

      Wasn't holding my past against me. The Lord was

      Implying also that I should forget about my past and Follow Jesus.

      **PHILIPPIANS 3:13-14, "Brethren, I do not count myself to have apprehended; but**

**one thing I do, forgetting those things which are behind and reaching forward to those things which are ahead, I press toward the goal for the Prize of the upward call of God in Christ Jesus."**

At the time of this writing many events and people have come into my life. I have the sense of being called into two areas of the five-fold ministry, prophet and pastor. Am I a pastoring prophet or a prophetic pastor? I guess time will tell as I trust the Holy Spirit to confirm His call upon my life.

# EPILOGUE

We are all at a different place in our spiritual growth and relationship with the Holy Spirit. I chose to share this adventure of my life hoping it will encourage you to go after the Holy Spirit and grow in your relationship with Him. I don't see myself as anybody great or extraordinary. I am just a regular person with a heart for God. I have committed myself to him to be whatever he wants me to be and go where ever He wants me to go. It's been an adventure and a journey.

# ABOUT THE AUTHOR

# BIO

William carries the anointing of a prophet and psalmist. He is also a Bible teacher, author and international speaker. He operates in all of the Spiritual gifts. He uses the gifts as the Holy Spirit wills. One of William's great desires is to lead others to Christ and to follow Holy Spirit wherever He leads.

YOU CAN VISIT MY WEBSITE
WWW.PSALMISTWILLIAM.CA
FOR ENCOURAGING PSALMS AND TO BUY OTHER BOOKS I HAVE WRITTEN

www.ingramcontent.com/pod-product-compliance
Lightning Source LLC
Chambersburg PA
CBHW031414040426
42444CB00005B/564